Geoffrey was born in East London in 1948 and grew up with his parents and two brothers in Winchmore Hill. He attended St Pauls C of E Primary School and, having failed his 11+, moved on to Winchmore Secondary Modern School. Here, he studied for his O and A Level GCEs before taking up a place at City University to read Civil Engineering. A career with Consulting Engineers and contractors but primarily Local Government served him well and, now retired, he lives with his wife in Buckinghamshire.

In memory of my dear friend, Judy, with whom I shared many a laugh in the Vestry!

Geoffrey Ring

MORE MUSINGS ON FAITH BY AN ORDINARY BLOKE

AUSTIN MACAULEY PUBLISHERS
LONDON ∘ CAMBRIDGE ∘ NEW YORK ∘ SHARJAH

Copyright © Geoffrey Ring 2024

The right of Geoffrey Ring to be identified as author of this work has been asserted by the author in accordance with sections 77 and 78 of the Copyright, Designs and Patents Act 1988.

All rights reserved. No part of this publication may be reproduced, stored in a retrieval system, or transmitted in any form or by any means, electronic, mechanical, photocopying, recording, or otherwise, without the prior permission of the publishers.

Any person who commits any unauthorised act in relation to this publication may be liable to criminal prosecution and civil claims for damages.

The story, experiences, and words are the author's alone.

A CIP catalogue record for this title is available from the British Library.

ISBN 9781035878529 (Paperback)
ISBN 9781035878536 (ePub e-book)

www.austinmacauley.com

First Published 2024
Austin Macauley Publishers Ltd®
1 Canada Square
Canary Wharf
London
E14 5AA

Table of Contents

Introduction	9
The Listening Ear	12
It Pays to Be Honest!	16
Peter	18
Wot…No Vicar ?	21
Changing Times	23
In Praise of Clergy	27
Don't Mention Death	29
Here We Go Again…	33
DON'T BLAME GOD!!	*33*
Explain This If You Can	35
Keeping in Touch	39
Was That the Beginning?	41
Slow Down!	44
Love One Another!	46

I Wonder What He Thinks Now?	**50**
Reflection on Mark Chapter 1 Verses 1–8	**53**
I Weep	**57**
Hard Lessons	**59**
A Little Bit of Homework!	**62**
Epilogue	**66**

Introduction

Language often weak	20/40
This is not a sentence; always answer in sentences	5½/20
Be careful of your choice of vocabulary	8/25
Never use 'also' as a join – See me before repeating You have been told not to use 'so' as a join., Quite good	11/20
Flashes of good writing to show what you can do. Keep on trying	15/40
There is promise here	16+/40
You are trying hard	16/40
And finally…	
Very well tried	11/25

Such ran the comments of my literary achievements from good old Mrs Phair, my English teacher in the 60s. Not overly encouraging as you can see but eventually I did seem to be 'trying very hard' although it still only merited 16/40! It certainly didn't suggest I should take up a career in writing did it?

Imagine my amazement when, 60 years later, I submitted a manuscript to publishers and it was received with great positivity, and my first book *"Musings on Faith by an Ordinary Bloke"* was on the shelves in your local bookstore. Obviously, no 'Mrs Phairs' on the review panel there!

But what did all this make me wonder? Perhaps those hours and hours spent over the years drafting literally hundreds of committee reports encouraging councillors to adopt various proposals had, in the end, been worthwhile, despite so many of those missives failing to win them over at the time. Perhaps all that work during a career in Local Government had honed my skills. You just never know what it is that will finally prove to be beneficial. And so it is with faith!

Have you ever been put off in the past from following anything religious? Were those around you scathing of any suggestions that there was a God 'up there'? Perhaps your RE (or RI as it was in my day) teacher was not the coolest person to be seen listening to. As the years passed did bad things happen to you, convincing you that believing was a waste of time? But rest assured that even if such things happened to you there is hope! Sometimes it takes a lifetime to fully appreciate what faith really has to offer. And it really does have so much. (Not sure whether this is a proper sentence, Mrs Phair, sorry).

The encouraging news is that my first book appears to have been bought by more people out there than I could ever have imagined. People, like you I guess, were tempted to maybe reflect on whether this faith lark, and thoughts about

God, weren't just for vicars, worthy churchgoers or religious cranks but ordinary folk. Ordinary folk who were looking for a greater meaning to life than just existing and surviving the daily run-of-the-mill problems one always faces.

Why not join them? It could change your life, just read on.

The Listening Ear

We've all been there, just looking for someone with whom we could unload our troubles. Someone who would just listen, not judge or offer advice, be empathetic, not sympathetic and be prepared to focus on us and not drift into their own experiences. Someone who would not interrupt, perhaps give the occasional nod and show that they were really listening. Someone we could trust with our troubles and know they were not going to be spread around. Someone who understood confidentiality and didn't think that that just meant being able to share it all with others 'confidentially'.

Whilst listening they may just ask "…and how does that feel?" or "…have you ever felt this way before?" to allow you to open up and explain exactly what the problem is. Find someone like that and they are like gold dust. "Why?" I hear you ask. Because a true listener enables you to realise that you do know what you need to do. You do know how to go on. You do know, deep down, that you can overcome whatever issues confront you. We all just need to have the space to speak openly, in confidence, about things we may never have vocalised before. We seldom know the way to cope until we can do this.

But there is a problem. Where can we find such a person with whom we feel comfortable enough? Yes, there are helplines available but it takes a degree of courage to pick up the phone and ask.

But there is someone always close by and waiting to hear about your troubles. No need to pick up the phone, no need to worry about your feelings being broadcast, no worries about upsetting a friend, just a perfect One awaiting your 'call'. Who? Well, it's God.

No, I haven't lost the plot or gone all religious, I'm just saying what I have found. He's always there and is the perfect listener. No one could be more understanding and, above all, confidential. What is bizarre is that it's even easier these days. Let me explain. When you are out and about, you often pass folk who seem to be talking to themselves. Mad? No just look for the earpiece and mobile. They are talking to friends ordering food and speaking aloud as if they were there. So, here is your answer. To avoid looking as if you have lost the plot just pop in an earpiece, hide the end of the wire in your pocket and talk to God.

Use Him as the perfect listener. As I have said earlier, somewhere, deep down, we do have the answers and we just need someone to listen as we go through the explanations of why we are feeling as we are or what it is that has hurt us. You can just imagine Him asking how you really feel, how you have coped in the past, what would make things better and tell Him. He will not interrupt or hijack the conversation, a perfect listener.

"It will never work," I hear you say, but trust me it will. Even a simple example came to mind as I was writing this that I recalled from my working days. It was not at a time I was in distress but when I was able to help a colleague without realising it. They were not distressed or in crisis, they just had a simple problem that needed solving. I had recently been promoted and now had the responsibility, amongst too many other things, for Woodland Management. Something I knew nothing about. One day, my Woodland's manager knocked at the door of my office with some sort of contraption that measured trees or the density of trees in a wood, I really can't remember what it was and certainly had never seen one before; neither had I any idea how it worked. She said she was having trouble working out how to use it but needed to go forth to the woods on a survey. Would I help? With the usual confidence of a boss who likes to give the impression of knowing what he is doing, I invited her in and said of course I could.

She started to explain what it did and how it helped in her survey work and the development of the Woodland Management Plan that she had been tasked to produce. With mild panic, I asked a few questions, showed interest, and wondered how all this would end and if my credibility would survive. Well, after about 15 minutes she put the instrument away and as she left, turned and said, "Thank you, that's a lot clearer and you must come for a tour of the Woodlands one day," which I gratefully accepted and did a few weeks later. Whilst on that trip, she showed me how the instrument I had 'helped' her to understand worked. I still to this day don't know what I'd said in that office, or what I'd not said about something I knew nothing about. I'd just listened, offered support, agreed and in the end, she had solved the problem herself. I think that deep down she knew the answers but just needed someone to listen, someone to vocalise her thoughts to and someone who wasn't going to launch in with unhelpful comments.

I know this may sound like a very insignificant example but it does show that just having someone to listen to you can really help no matter how small or serious the problem. Why not try it? He's waiting for your call right now.

It Pays to Be Honest!

Asleep at last, he thought to himself
As he crept out of the children's room.
But as he got to the door, from under the covers,
A little voice he heard…
"Daddy."
"Yes darling," he said with a sigh,
No supper yet, he thought
"Mummy says Grandma has gone to heaven, what's Heaven like?"
Not only no supper, he realised quite soon
No evening as well, it would seem.
He knew he'd tried normal responses before
To questions just like this.
The 'Ask Mummy tomorrow' and 'It's time you were asleep' never worked.
A new strategy was needed, but would it work now
Or lead to a lengthy debate?
But he'd try it, fingers crossed and launched into what he believed Heaven was like.
Would it work or land him in trouble?
There was only one way to find out.

"It's a place where there is no hatred or strife,
Where love and happiness are always rife
Where we meet up again with friends that we knew
Where we see them as remembered
When they were here too.
Where time stands still, there's no ageing or wear,
Just peace, and tranquillity, and friendships to share.
Where we will not argue or try to score points
But exist alongside others in harmony.
No racial or class discrimination there.
We understand at last the true meaning of life,
What it was all about,
But we still watch over those that we've left behind,
Talk to them and hope they can hear.
That's Heaven."

Then there was silence, what had he just said?
Where had it come from so long in his head.?
He waited in trepidation but then a voice said,

"Thank you, Daddy, good night, and God bless."

He knew now that what he just thought was so true,
That God moves in mysterious ways.
Just speak the truth, be brave and with confident faith
Even children can sleep soundly again!

Peter

Hi, my name is Peter, or that's the name that everybody seems to know me by now. I used to be known as Simeon, or sometimes Simon, until I met Jesus. When I met Him, he called me Cephas, which came from the Aramaic Kepa and means rock. It's even more complicated than that! The Greek translation of Kepa is Petros, hence Peter. I was born in Bethsaida in Galilee where I lived with my brother Andrew. Together we went into the fishing business with our friends James and John.

It's difficult to remember how exactly when we met Jesus or perhaps I should say He met us. We must have been in our late teens or early 20s and were on the beach about to start fishing by the lake of Galilee and He just appeared. He seemed like a nice chap but there was something about Him that made Him a bit special. Can't really put my finger on it but it was there. One of His first comments as we were chatting was, *"Follow me and I will make you fishers of men"*[1]. I don't think any of us really understood what it meant then; it was only later that things began to become clearer.

---

[1] Matthew Chapter 4 Verse 19

Amazingly, we did pack up our nets and join Him on what was to be an extraordinary journey. There were highs and lows, despair and exhilaration over the years. He assembled 12 of us to help Him with His ministry and He gave me the honour of being a sort of leader of the group. Little did we know in those early days, how it was all going to end. He tried to give us a few hints as the years went by but I don't think we really understand what He was telling us.

I have to admit that there were often times when I didn't understand a lot of things. Some of the parables that He told His followers I didn't always follow. I sometimes wonder whether there were others who didn't either. Having said that, they always made you think and perhaps that was the whole point.

I always tried to listen, stay calm, and support Jesus all I could. I have to admit that sometimes I was a bit rash and hasty but always tried to be loyal and faithful. There was only once when I really let myself down, and I mean really. It was just after Jesus had been arrested in the Garden and we had fled in all directions. I went to a local pub to try and come to terms with what had happened and someone shouted out that I was one of His followers. I was so scared, so said I wasn't again and again and again. Then a cock crowd and I realised what I had done. It was just as Jesus had predicted. I was so ashamed and have never really come to terms with what I did. Jesus, being Jesus, never mentioned it again and appeared to us all a few times without any recriminations, that was how He was. Perhaps I was forgiven, I hope so.

I was about 50 when all that happened and looking back now on the incredible journey we had had together since our teenage years is a humbling experience. I'm about 65 now and not sure how long it will be before the authorities plan my demise. We shall see!

Wot...No Vicar ?

Who is this chap standing up front and telling us all what to do?
To sit and to stand to sing and to pray, who does he think that he is?
I came to this church to hear from the Vicar, for surely that's who we pay.?
And here is this bloke, no collar or robes; I really don't know what to say

But I'm up near the front, can't slip away now so better just sit here and bear it,
I suppose it is different but is it allowed, presumably he's no formal training.
Just a bloke, a bit like me, seems a nice chap; I wonder how this will play out.
Surely, it can't be a real church service but wait, what was it I read?
Today was to be lay lead, but I didn't know what that meant.
Perhaps this is it then, led by a chap and not by an expert as usual.

But now he is going to give us a sermon based on the
reading we heard.
But he's calling it reflection, this should be interesting,
for how, untrained, can he possibly explain it, when I'm
still puzzling at what it all meant?
But wait, he's now saying it confused him as well, good
for him but how can that help?
He's gone on to say that he struggles sometimes but tells
what he thinks it all means
What message the writer was trying to give, whether
he'd understood it like that or not.
And do you know what, I agree with him now for I'd
thought that myself at the time

Now the church I remember with ladies in hats and
gloves on more often than not.
With gents in best suits and children kept quiet and
vicars most definitely men.
The church that I left, for I didn't feel part, I think now
has changed for the better.
I might come again but hopefully then,
I'll meet with the vicar in person!

Changing Times

I realised the other day that so many words, phrases, cultures, and meanings have changed, even in our short lifetimes that it is not surprising that so much of the Bible's teachings are so hard to understand.

To children, and even many adults, what they think they understand is not what was meant. Take a couple of simple examples. When I was a lad at Sunday school, we often sang the hymn:

"There is a green hill far away
Without a city wall."

I could never understand why we were singing about a green hill that didn't have a city wall. It was ages before I came to realise that the green hill was outside the city wall and not that it didn't have one! At one Sunday school, I remember we had a talk about death. Looking back, a seemingly strange subject. All I can imagine is that someone had died and the poor teacher had been given the task of saying a few words about life after death. All I remember is that she said that our souls went to heaven. Other things were said in the lesson and at the end, we were allowed to do some drawings about what we had learnt. Whilst one does not remember much about those sorts of details of one's childhood, I vividly remember what I drew. It was something like this:

I'm not sure what was said about it but I don't recall any adverse comments. It wasn't long before I began to realise that that possibly was not what she meant!

Another was the comment in the Bible where Jesus said:

"Suffer the little children to come unto me[2]…"

---

[2] Mark Chapter 10 Verse 14 (Authorised King James Version)

Why would children want to follow what Jesus said if they had to suffer? I thought. However, fortunately, in later versions, it was re-translated as:

"Let the little children come to me, do not stop them…"[3]

Which made a lot more sense. Well, it obviously didn't put me off too much in starting my journey of faith all those years ago. There are the amusing stories, of course, where children do not hear exactly what is said. Like the answer one gave in an RE test saying:

"Christians only have one wife and it's called monotony."

Having been together now with my wife for over 50 years, I can certainly disagree with that sentiment!

What I am trying to say is that we must try and look behind some of the biblical texts, whether they are stories, predictions, parables, or miracles to fully understand what their true meanings were. It was such a different age when they were written and we have to take that into account. There are some practices of the time we read about that are obviously 'of the era' and not for today. There are others, which may sound the same but at that time meant something different.

There are many long books written on this subject but if you feel like delving further, I would recommend John Hargreaves – *A Guide to The Parables*[4]. It is probably out of print now but if you can find a copy; I think you will find it

---

[3] Mark Chapter 10 Verse 14 (New Revised Standard Version)
[4] Published in 1968 by S.P.C.K., made and printed by Knight & Forster Ltd, London

interesting. It's a guide to the interpretation of the 12 parables he has chosen by considering the original situation and then seeing it in our own situation.

Or, of course, you could just read my poem *"Nobody said it would be easy"* [5].

Happy days…

---

[5] Musings on Faith by an Ordinary Bloke – published 2024

In Praise of Clergy

The church was packed at Christmas and at Easter just the same.
The vicar did her duties and pointed out the aim.
Spoke about the message, and gave all a good insight.
It all went down so well, to everyone's delight.
They mingled and they chatted, had lots and lots to say,
Then left the church together to continue with their day.
But when they'd gone, I thought a while
And realised that I ought
To praise again our clergy, but not for what they taught.
For things, they never say that must surely cross their mind
To point out to those present, if they're ever so inclined,
To call in again, for we'll always be here
There's a welcome for you and lots of good cheer.
But not a word is said after any oration
When they preach to a full and engrossed congregation
And know that next week there'll be but a few,
Always hoping there'll be a new one or two.
Preaching the Word, spreading His news
If only to just a keen few in the pews.
They're a credit to God who called them all up
Knowing they'd do a fine job.

So next time you meet one, remember to say
Thank you so much for your work every day.
But don't be downhearted come sunshine or rain
For one day, your church will fill up again.

Don't Mention Death

I realised the other day that there are so many unknowns during our lives, from school through our teens and adulthood. We never quite know what we will end up doing, what professions we'll have, how successful we will be and how our lives will pan out. During the passing of the years, we probably have endless discussions about all of these things and try to take on board others' views and experiences they might have had. Why is it then that the one thing we can all agree upon is the one issue very seldom discussed and that is that one day we will die? Obviously, we hope that it will be later rather than sooner, but we can rest assured that it is something that we will all have to face one day.

In musing on this, I wondered why it is that death is so rarely discussed. Is it because people feel that discussing it is 'tempting fate' and that it will hasten its arrival? Is it that talking about it is somewhat morbid and you just don't do it? Is it that if we discuss it, we just don't know what to say about it? Is it that if we discuss it with someone who is ailing in some way it might be perceived as saying, "You won't be here much longer"?

In pondering all this, it seemed right to try and put on paper my thoughts, which you never know, might help someone somewhere to broach the subject in a more positive and less embarrassing way.

As I said, death will come to all of us. The only unknown is when. I think it will be like the park keeper, who used to look after the rowing boats on Groveland's Park Lake, who used to shout out, "Come in number 36, your time is up!" and this will be God's call when our time is up. But what is death? Is it the end or the beginning?

Now without getting too evangelical, heaven forbid, I need to quote from the Bible one of the most famous of Jesus' comments[6], which went:

"I am the resurrection and the life. Those who believe in me, even though they die, will live, and everyone who lives and believes in me will never die. Do you believe this?"

Wow, now that is something that needs some thought. I guess He is not saying that if you have faith and believe in Him, that you will live the life as you know it forever. No, what this tells us is that the life we know is only the beginning and there is another life to follow. What that will be like no one really knows but it is comforting to think that death is not the end.

To try and get one's head around this and begin to understand whether that can possibly be true, I would put the following to you. Life on Earth has been going on for millennia. We, however, are only here for the blink of an eye in comparison. As is said at many funeral services:

---

[6] John Chapter 11 Verses 25 and 26

"For we brought nothing into this world, and it is certain we can carry nothing out."[7]

On this basis, apart from doing what we can whilst we are here to leave this world a better place than when we joined it, perhaps there is more to life. Perhaps it is all a preparation for the next one.

But I do feel that there are two main things that might worry many about death. The first is not actually death but dying. Will it hurt, will it be quick? Will I suffer for long and some such questions? There is also the worry some folk have as to how those left behind will cope.

Let's start with the first question. Obviously, if a heart attack strikes, you will probably know little about it. There are stories of people waking up in the morning and finding their partner had died in the night, again, very quickly. On the other hand, if you find yourself with a long terminal prognosis then worries could set in. But, knowing how palliative care has developed since the first hospice opened in London in the 1960s, and with the introduction of more effective medication, pain should not be an issue.

Finally, there is the concern as to how those left behind in the life you once knew would cope. Here, I'm afraid, is where faith comes in. Sorry. I firmly believe that when the good Lord calls out your number and off you go to join Him, He will take care of those yet to be called. He will give them the strength to cope with their loss, the confidence to undertake things that previously they may not have done, help them find ways to deal with their grief and generally be at their side as

---

[7] 1 Timothy Chapter 6 verse 7

the months go by. Rest assured, He will not leave them alone. This should be a great comfort to you when knowing you will soon have to leave them behind.

As I have said before, my 'musings' are what I believe and may not register with other folk. However, I do hope that in some small way, such views may prompt wider discussions about these things and enable some to speak more freely about what they do or don't believe. Do let me know via my publishers if you wish to open any discussions about any of the areas covered.

In the meantime, God Bless.

Here We Go Again…

As we open the papers, switch on the news and watch the television reports it is no wonder that there is a temptation to cry out aloud "Where is God in all this?" The wars, knife crime, violence on the street, racism and much more, it is all so depressing. But I always turn to some thoughts I had which featured as a poem in my first book[8]. As so little seems to have improved since then, and may even have got worse, I make no apologies for featuring that poem again here. It bears the title:

DON'T BLAME GOD!!

When we look at the world and see hunger and strife
Hatred, violence, and killings so rife.
When we hear in the news of anger and war
With people not talking but shouting much more.
We wonder sometimes where God is in all this.
But wait.

---

[8] Musings on Faith by an Ordinary Bloke, Published in 2024 by Austin Macauley

Never let your faith ever start to dim, and certainly never begin to blame Him.
Just remember:
He gave us brains so as that we could choose
Whether to love or dislike,
Whether to hear or just listen
Whether to comfort others or just ignore their plight.
Whether to grow food in plenty to share or just look on as others go without.
Whether to develop science to help save lives or just plan destruction.
Whether to put the environment first or let big business take the lead.
Whether to think before we act or just rush in.
So when things seem to be going wrong or bad things beginning to happen
It's probably because the choices made with the brains that He gave us are perhaps the reason and not the fault of God
He is always there, we just need to use and not abuse the gifts He gave us.
Hopefully, this will bring some peace of mind to those who begin to question their faith, it certainly does mine.

Explain This If You Can

This morning I wanted to venture into the impossible! How many times in church have we heard the phrase "Father, Son, and Holy Spirit"? Despite hearing it so often it is one of the most difficult things to try and get your head around. In fact, many don't even worry about it and carry on saying it without trying to get to grips with the concept of The Trinity, for that is what this trio is called. The line in the hymn *"Holy, Holy, Holy"* sums it up when we sing:

"God in three Persons, blessed Trinity!"

The confusion for me resulted from so many conflicting statements in the Bible about 'these three', who were, in fact, One. In the Old Testament, life seemed a lot more straightforward with most references to God just as The Father. An example being in Isaiah[9] where he states:

"For you are our Father, though Abraham does not know us and Israel does not acknowledge us; you, O Lord, are our Father; our Redeemer from of old is your name."

---

[9] Isaiah Chapter 63 Verse 16

However, with the arrival of Jesus in the New Testament the confusion begins. If you look at some of the passages in the Bible, you will read a description of when Jesus said:

"I and the Father are one."[10]

Now, He may not literally mean that He and the Father are one but just that they're 'on the same wavelength'. Maybe a bit like saying to a colleague, when you agree on something "We are one on that." Of course, He may be getting folks prepared for the day when He is God.

I suppose the only analogy you could use to try and explain how two things could exist as one, or move back and forth from one thing to another is to consider a quantity of water. Let's pretend that God is the water. At first, He is known as God the Father, just one entity. On the arrival of Jesus, the Son, it's as if some of the water has changed into something else, let's say ice. The water is still there but in a different form. "But they cannot exist together?" I hear you say, either it is water or ice. But hold on a minute. If I freeze just some of my water and put the resultant ice cubes back into the water, they will exist with the water, two in one at the same time you might say.

But things get even more complicated when, having been raised from the dead, and spotted by Mary after His resurrection, He says to her:

---

[10] John Chapter 10 Verse 30

"Do not hold on to me, for I have not yet ascended to the Father."[11]

Just before His ascension, He says to His disciples:

"I came from the Father and entered the world; now I am leaving the world and going back to the Father."[12]

And soon after that, Luke reports:

"When he had led them out to the vicinity of Bethany, he lifted up his hands and blessed them. While he was blessing them, he left them and was taken up into heaven."[13]

But that's not the end of all the confusion. We not only refer to the Father and the Son but also the Holy Spirit. Now after the ascension we read in the book of Acts Chapter 2 Verses 1–5 that the disciples:

*"...saw what seemed to be tongues of fire that separated and came to rest on each of them. All of them were filled with the **Holy Spirit** and began to speak in other tongues as the Spirit enabled them. Now there were staying in Jerusalem, God-fearing Jews from every nation under heaven."*

Now we are meant to understand three in one. The Father, Son, and Holy Spirit. Here again, the water and ice analogy holds true. If we take our water and ice and heat them up what

---

[11] John Chapter 20 Verse 17

[12] John Chapter 16 Verse

[13] Luke Chapter 24 Verses 50–51

happens? The ice melts, but the water is still there. Then water boils and turns to steam and we have the Holy Spirit. The water and ice are one with the steam and it is the steam that envelopes us just like the Holy Spirit. It is all we can see and then that itself disperses and we are left to believe that it was once water, then ice and then steam. *That,* I think, *is faith.*

But wait a moment, and please don't be put off religion if all this just confuses you more and certainly doesn't help you understand the concept of The Trinity. It is not always necessary to fully understand things but to still be able to gain a tremendous amount from them.

There have been many things that I have not fully understood in my life but have still been able to benefit from. A case in point, I always recall, are my maths lessons at school! I could never grasp the concept of calculus or understand what the point of it was. However, I did know that if I was asked the differentiate $2x$ the answer was 2 and the integral of 2 was $2x$ + a constant. This did get a lot more complicated but formulae and processes could be learnt to get one through it all. Get through it I did with reasonable A Level GCE passes in both pure and applied maths. Did I really understand what it was all about? No. Did I feel that really mattered? No. Did it stop me from really enjoying my maths? No. I know most mathematicians would frown upon this approach, but I was never one of those. I therefore feel that not being an ecclesiastical guru and not really fully accepting the concept of The Trinity need stop you from getting real benefits from a strong Faith so please don't worry, don't let me confuse you and just read on…

Keeping in Touch

We know it's always difficult to keep in touch with friends.
Those we should make the effort for, but don't.
The ones for whom we write in a card whether
Christmas, birthday, or thanks
"Must try and pop and see you, next year perhaps."
But things get in the way be they family, children or work.
The time goes by and it never seems right to make the space to go.
But then, we do eventually feel that waiting is no longer fair, so off we go to brave the traffic, weather and unknown reception.
And isn't it good, how great we feel having caught up with all the news.
To have spent that time to share with them, that time we didn't have.
And how much easier after that having broken the ice again to visit more often and keep in touch and rekindle that friendly flame.
But church, you know, is just the same; yes, things get in the way

The children's sport and camps, and clubs the endless work brought home
There's just not time to make that visit to pop to your local church.
But once the ice is broken again, just as you found before you meet those folk waiting for you to offer support and friendship.
But wait, it is not only them just willing you to visit, for God is waiting just for you to be there when you need Him.
To re-kindle that old flame or nurture anew to be there when times get tough.
As with your friend, it's easier then having broken the ice to go forward to pop in again, to keep in touch, and to develop a faith within you.
So delay it no longer, it's handily near and open for most of the time.
You may be surprised at what you will gain and for once, it won't cost you a dime.

Was That the Beginning?

It was the 3rd of July 1963 when they set off. Two Boy Scouts, one aged 15 and the other 13, laden with rucksacks, tent, map, compass, cooking gear, sealed instruction and a degree of trepidation. It was to be the older boy's last test before being awarded his First Class Badge. The younger one was his responsibility and for him, it was a practice before having to do the same thing himself a few years later. In full Scout uniform, which having passed the relevant tests included a sheath knife in his belt, how things have changed, and not really knowing where they were headed, they boarded the train at their local railway station. It was a time when parents were happy for 15- and 13-year-olds to go off by themselves for the weekend without knowing their destination or exactly when they would be back. No mobile phones to keep in touch then.

On the train, they opened their sealed instructions. It gave them the map references of the route they were to follow, no SatNavs in those days, the tasks they had to perform and an indication as to where they might find somewhere suitable to camp for the night. This would certainly not be a registered campsite or an Air B&B. This would be a friendly farmer's field who wouldn't mind two lads camping on his land and lighting a fire to cook their supper.

The hike went well and they managed to find that friendly farmer for the night. He offered them a barn to stay in, but "No" they said, they had to camp out! The tent was pitched, wood was found for the fire, supper was cooked and then it was time to snuggle down in their sleeping bags for a well-deserved rest. So far so good…

In the early hours of the morning, the intense rain seemed to have eased a little with only the thunder and lightning remaining. The tent was awash, sleeping bags soaked and two very frightened boys were suddenly awake. A quick check outside indicated that their tent pitching had stood up to the storm but the farmer's field had not. It was like a lake. But they were scouts and not going to give up. They decided it was better to be inside wet sleeping bags than trying to keep warm outside them. Uncomfortably, they eased down into the sodden bags. Suddenly, the older boy wondered if he would be able to last the night like this, despite reassuring his young friend that all would be well. He began to panic and then, unexpectedly, cried out:

"If I didn't believe in God before. I do now!"

And he recited the Lord's Prayer out aloud. What his friend thought I can't imagine. Well, did it help? Only you, the reader, can decide. But what I can tell you is that they did go off to sleep and were awakened the next morning by a voice outside. It was the farmer's wife with the words, "Good morning, I've brought you a cup of tea, a bit of a wet night, are you okay?"

How wonderful was that? They enjoyed their tea and accepted the invitation this time to go into the barn to dry out, get dressed, have breakfast, and head off on their way. That scout always remembered the first time he called to God for help. Perhaps that was the real start of a long journey of faith even if he didn't realise it at the time.

By the way, he submitted his hike report to his Scout Master, had an interview with the District Commissioner about it, passed the test, and was awarded his First Class Badge on 11th September 1963. He still has it 60 years later and often reflects on God's support all those years ago.

Slow Down!

Is it wrong to just slow down and give us time to think?
Do I need to know the news each minute for which I've no control?
Won't once a day or a daily paper suffice my appetite
And give me time to think some more about what surely matters?
Of all the things that we can control that really need our time.
The constant beeps, and clicks, and tunes emitting from our phones
And then we look and see it's Brian who has lost his dog again.
But Brian lives in Edinburg 500 miles away, so why tell me I doubt I'll see it passing through this way.
And what was it I was doing before that interruption?
I can't recall, never mind, let's start on something new.
And so life goes on with Brian's a-plenty telling me things I should know.
The news app's as bad with regular updates of another pending disaster.
But then I switched off and what do you know life took on something new,

I stopped worrying about Brian's dog, the news, and things I couldn't control.
I started to think of the things that mattered
The things important to me.
I started looking around when out for walks not waiting for the phone to sound.
The birds I heard, talked to those that I passed and appreciated all around.
It gave me time to think of things that sadly I'd forgotten
The friends and family I should call again not focus just on work
Those jobs at home I'd been putting off that could be sorted out so quickly.
But most of all, it gave me time to think of One again,
One absent for too long, drowned out by the pace of life.
One who now has space to be with me once more.
Yes God, I'm still here and pray that you will pardon my tweets, and beeps, and blogs and all that got in the way.
I've missed you so much but rest assured, I'm now here with you to stay.
And by the way, Brian found his dog hiding under the bed.
I didn't really need to know so I'll delete that news instead.

Love One Another!

This morning we heard about the time when John reported Jesus saying:

"A new command I give you: Love one another. As I have loved you, so you must love one another. By this, everyone will know that you are my disciples, if you love one another."[14]

Well, there are many challenges we face in life, some we rise to, some we shun and some we really try to face head-on. Some we succeed in, others not so. Here we were set a challenge to beat all challenges. Did Jesus really realise how difficult that would be for us mere mortals? I guess He probably did whilst also knowing that some of us would fail. But a challenge for all of us, it certainly was. I can look around this morning and see friends and colleagues with whom I have great respect, but would I say I loved any of you? Perhaps before we all start beating ourselves up about not loving each other or that person around the corner, or feeling an intimate connection with the family next door, let's take a closer look

---

[14] John Chapter 12 Verse 34

at what He really meant. In considering more carefully this commandment, we have to take into account the terminology or meanings of words of that era.

To start with, we need to understand how problematic translations can be from one language to another and then to another language altogether. I'm sure that those of you who have studied a foreign language can think of words or phrases in that language that you have struggled to give an accurate translation of when sitting those written tests.

We first hear about loving one another in the Old Testament in Leviticus[15] where it says:

"Love your neighbour as yourself."

But here we must remember that the Old Testament was originally written in Hebrew with some sections even in Aramaic. In many instances, the original Hebrew writings of the Old Testament included the word 'khesed', a word you will not find there today. It is one of the Hebrew words that, in some instances, has been translated to mean love. In fact, the word reflects not only a feeling but an action. Consequently, it is one of those words that do not really have a direct translation into English as it has a range of meanings. In fact, those who study these things for a living seem to say that it may appear around 250 times, mostly in the book of Psalms. However, having looked at all the examples given not one included the word. So what goes on? We come back to the problems of translation.

---

[15] Leviticus Chapter 19 Verse 18

The Hebrew word 'khesed' was translated in the early King John Version of the Bible as 'loving kindness' or 'mercy'. However, here again, the word itself does not appear. Theologian John Oswalt said the word means *"...a completely undeserved kindness and generosity."* To see some of the other translations, you can look at where it originally appeared in the Bible. For instance, in Genesis[16], it is translated as:

"...your servant has found favour with you, and you have shown me great kindness..."

And in Zachariah[17]:

"Render true judgements, show kindness and mercy to one another; do not oppress the widow, the orphan, the alien, or the poor; and do not devise evil in your hearts against one another."

Why am I going on about all these meanings and translations I hear you say? Well, perhaps it helps us to understand a little more clearly as to what *"Love your neighbour as yourself"* was really meant to mean. Perhaps we are not talking about what we refer to as love today, which tends to imply strong feelings of affection when referring to relationships with others. Perhaps Jesus is not saying we should have such affection for others but just to show them kindness, mercy, loyalty and generosity. Now, things begin to

---

[16] Genesis Chapter 19 Verse 19

[17] Zachariah Chapter 7 Verse 9

look a little more feasible. Not that even that makes it a great deal easier.

I'm sure we all set out with the best will in the world and good intentions to practise Khesed with our fellows, but how often do we find that it's just too difficult? I can recall times when I have felt it impossible to show such feelings to such an extent that for times, my Lord's Prayer had to be modified when I said it to:

*"...forgive us our trespasses **as we try so hard** to forgive them that trespass against us..."*

Fortunately, those periods didn't last long and I hope that God would have appreciated my weakness and understood my pain.

Perhaps it should be our mission this week to start spreading a little more Khesed around and doing our bit to make this a better world for all. Go on, I know you can do it!

Amen.

I Wonder What He Thinks Now?

He started out all by Himself with just 12 men to serve.
As time went by, His following grew and others came to help.
But all too young He had to leave, as was the plan always.
He left behind an active team, which spread the word both far and wide.
As decades passed and numbers grew to heights quite stratospheric, the structure felt by some as needed grew in similar ways.
No longer just those dedicated folk who worked to spread the word, but a managerial structure felt the need to guide them all as well.
So now, 2000 years have passed and what is it we have?
Not just those folk who spread the word but:

Archbishops
Diocesan Bishops
Suffragan Bishops
Archdeacons
Assistant Archdeacons
Rural Deans
Rectors

Vicars

Curates

Not forgetting the Cathedral set-up (Under the Bishop) comprising:

Deans

Precentors

Chancellors

Treasurers

Also in some Cathedrals:

Subdeans

Cannons

Vice-chancellors

But, of course, with such a structure, if things go wrong, there must be a system to investigate the wrongdoings which are covered by:

The Prerogative Court of the Archbishop

The Consistory Court of the Bishops

The Archdeaconry Court of the Archdeacons

The Decanal Courts of the Dean of an Exempt Deanery of the Cathedral

The Peculiar Courts of Cathedral Officials, Prebends, Parishes etc.

But that's not all we must not forget the few

Royal Peculiars and their associated Courts

But as He looks down upon us now does He puzzle at what we have done?

Did He foresee such a vast set-up to spread His simple words?

With houses and palaces and grand institutions,

With back-office staff and buildings to suit them.

With procedures, policies and strategic directions.

With scholarly interpretations of His teachings at Synod,
With hours in meetings with minutes that follow
But to me the key person in all this malaise, destined to serve Him the best.
Is the one who actually does all the work to keep His word spreading afar.
The one who has to relate to us all and fields the difficult questions.
The one with the knowledge of what really matters
To the differing congregations they serve.
Yes, you've guessed, for me at the top of the tree
The one that we all see every week.
It's our Vicar who is there and may God bless them all
For without them, the others would fall.

Reflection on Mark Chapter 1 Verses 1–8

This morning we heard the reading about John the Baptist and how he baptised many people from Jerusalem and the surrounding Judean countryside. But what seemed odd to me was the way that Mark highlighted what John was wearing and what he ate! He referred to clothing of camel's hair and eating honey and locusts. Why did Mark put that in his report? Seems odd to highlight what he was wearing and eating when the key story was about what he did and the message he was bringing. Or perhaps it was a way of highlighting, to those he wanted his report to resonate with, the fact that John the Baptist was not a grand chap with fancy clothes and wealthy friends but just an ordinary, hard-up, chap like them. Seeing that:

"The whole Judean countryside and all the people of Jerusalem went out to him."[18]

It would appear to have worked!

---

[18] Mark Chapter 1 Verse 5

Now I know that many ecclesiastical gurus may disagree with me, nothing new there, as they have speculated that these words from Mark were symbolic. He was saying that the food going into John's mouth represented the message coming out of his mouth, with those who received John's message with faith tasting its sweetness and experiencing God's blessing, like honey, and those refusing John's message experiencing God's judgment, like locusts. I could possibly go along with this if it was Jesus giving one of His parables with a deeper meaning. But this was Mark reporting on what he had witnessed and I think that it was more likely that it was for the reason I mentioned.

However, the key issue was that many people saw something important to their faith in the act of baptism as a way of repentance and forgiveness of their sins. Over the years, there seems to have been a degree of confusion between christenings and baptisms. I know from my point of view having attended many, both for the family and at other church services, I always used to call them christenings. Most of the greetings and congratulation cards in shops for these occasions tended to be worded as christenings. But gradually more appeared as baptisms and generally, the words were interchangeable. But are they? Having looked a little further into this recently, I now realise that there is a key difference, reinforcing the motto that it is never too late to learn!

I now understand that a christening need not involve a baptism. How odd is that? The word christening comes from the old English word christen, which means 'to name', and that is what christening is, naming the child. Baptism is an invitation to join the Church family that welcomes the new member and will help support them on their faith journey.

Baptism forgives all sin and makes the baptised person a child of God and a member of God's family. The Holy Spirit is given at baptism to help the newly baptised live a faithful Christian life.

When a baby or young child is baptised, the parents accept the invitation on behalf of their child. Older children and adults accept the invitation themselves. There are many symbols in the act of baptism. Water in the font is blessed by the vicar and is then used as a symbol of life. In baptism, Christ gives new life.

I will pause at this stage to recall a moment in my life when my understanding, as I thought, of baptism was shattered! I must have been about seven or eight and had seen a number of baptisms or christenings, as I called them then. The golden jug that this magical water was poured from, which I presumed had been flown in, especially from the River Jordon, always spellbound me. One day I was coming into the church and I saw one of the churchwardens with this golden jug ready for pouring the magical water into the font. They then proceeded to fill it up from the tap outside…my world fell apart! It was a bit like being backstage and seeing how the conjurer did his trick; I was mortified. It was some years before I came to fully understand that it was the blessing of the water, the ordinary water, that made it Holy and then used as a symbol of life. The moral here, I think, is not to assume children understand what we think they do, talk to them and explain what it all means wherever possible.

To continue. Having poured the water over the infant's head with the accompanying sentences, Holy Oil, a symbol of strength and healing, is used to make the sign of the cross on the baby's forehead. It's a symbol that the baby has the gift of the Holy Spirit and has been made holy, a special friend of Jesus who is king. Finally, a lighted candle is given as a sign that Jesus is the light of the world.

I know that many of you will say, "But how can a baby take all this in?" and that is why parents ask Godparents to help them as the child is growing up. Godparents support parents in the faith development of the child being baptised. At the child's baptism, parents and Godparents answer on behalf of the child and agree to nurture their development in the Christian life. Being a Godparent is about being a role model in the life of faith. They are also present to represent the Church family of which the baptised is becoming part. Godparents take an active role in helping the parents nurture their child's faith.

Some parents feel that they are not able, in all honesty, to take on this role and there is nothing wrong with that. It may be that they feel that they do not have the strength of faith needed to make the promises in front of the congregation or to themselves. What is important is that they leave the door open for their children, as they grow up, to make the decision themselves to be baptised. I heard of a case recently where a 14-year-old had asked their parents if they could be baptised. They had obviously heard something, learned about faith, or felt a calling, one can only speculate but they now felt able to make the commitment themselves without placing that responsibility on their parents.

I think the message here is that it is never too late to find faith. It sometimes happens at the most odd times.

God Bless

I Weep

I weep when I listen to news,
Of the things that we have done
To spoil this wonderful world
Once the home of your Son.
We fight, argue, and hear of the wars
That leaders launch with seldom a pause.
We see the anguish and terror first-hand
That results from the violence, we can't understand.
Can they not see what's bound to arise
When the battles are over, is it such a surprise?
Is there never a thought of another way forward,
Where there is room for peace and reflection?
A way that moves from death and destruction
Nearer to goodwill and affection.
Of course, it's not easy dealing with those
Who thrive on acts such as terror;
The ones who won't listen or talk but just fight
And thrive on the chaos they cause.
Perhaps we should ask ourselves why is it
That they act in such terrible ways.
Is there history there that still lurks deep down
In the feelings of many today?

Is it that that's the key to finding a way
To try and start a new era.
An era where wars will no longer be fought
And talking replaces the weapons.
We can but hope and pray
That it will be so some day
And God will look down and eventually say,
"At last, they've got it, hooray!"

Hard Lessons

There are times when you come face to face with faith and are sorely tested. It is at such times that I hear my old Chief Executive's voice ringing in my ears. I had just been promoted to the post of Director of Technical Services within a local authority. One day, having struggled with an issue I can't even remember, I popped into his office to 'unload'. He listened for a while and then proclaimed, "Nobody said it would be easy!" and it certainly wasn't. But the same goes for faith, which is sometimes also very testing; times when despite prayers what you pray for doesn't seem to happen. But strangely enough, it is times like that when we can learn lessons that actually strengthen our faith.

Let me give you one such example that happened to me. I was probably in my mid-twenties and working as a Senior Assistant Engineer within a small local authority. I had a good friend in the office; let's call him Stuart[19]. He was the same age as me and also had young children as we did. He was a great guy with whom I used to play bowls in the Works Bowls League. One day, he came into the office complaining of a pain in his stomach. After a while, he decided he should visit

---

[19] Not his real name

the doctor and left the office to go and see him. The doctor immediately sent him directly to the hospital for the diagnosis he feared.

The next, we heard was that Stuart had been diagnosed with advanced cancer of the liver and was sent home with approximately six weeks to live. I was absolutely gutted. Just like Stuart, he did pop back into the office to say he didn't really feel like finishing the project drawings he was working on and, not surprisingly, nobody disagreed with that.

What followed was the experience that I had during the following weeks and, yes, the six weeks was correct. For the first time in my life, I actually knelt by my bed each night and prayed so sincerely that Stuart's life would be spared and he be allowed to see his children grow up. When he died six weeks later, I wondered why my prayers had not been answered. Had I done something wrong, had I asked for the impossible? In the weeks that followed I did not have an answer to those questions, just sadness.

It was many years later that I began to realise that my pleas to God were misplaced and instead of asking for a miracle my prayer should have been:

*Dear Lord, I know You **can** either heal Stuart or prepare a place for him with You. I pray that you will be with those around him and give them all that they need to cope with whatever is planned for him.*

We should not be trying to 'test' God, for He is the One who tests us. What I eventually came to realise is that in calling Stuart to His side, He did provide all the strength and fortitude that was needed by those left behind. They were able to move forward. His wife had been given instructions from Stuart before he died to feel free to marry again, as long as it wasn't to an estate agent or car salesman! She did find a new partner who 'met the criteria' and has now been happily married for many years. The children have grown up, married and, seeing the marriage photos, the groom now looks so much like his father that it brings all those memories back to me. In some strange way, that episode in my life really strengthened my relationship with God, I don't know why; after all, He didn't do what I'd asked! Perhaps it was that really intense prayer, the certain knowledge I felt that He was there to listen and the sort of relationship one has with a true counsellor who is there to just listen and not interrupt. I don't know why it had such a positive effect on my faith journey but I know someone who does!

Why not see what He can do for you?

A Little Bit of Homework!

For those who have actually managed to get to the end of both my books, I thought you deserved a little homework! Most folks are aware that the Bible is split into two halves, the first being The Old Testament and the second The New Testament. However, few realise that, sandwiched in between we find the Apocrypha. What a wonderful word that is. It contains books with fascinating titles like Tobit, Maccabees, and Esdras. I have always been intrigued as to where it came from and why its books did not warrant places in either the Old or New Testaments. Needless to say, as with a lot of ecclesiastical mysteries, there is a wealth of literature, essays, books, and theses that have been written on the subject and I certainly don't intend to try and compete with any of them here.

What I wanted to do was look just a little further into what has intrigued me over the years and see whether I could come up with an 'ordinary bloke's' view as a tempter for you to do more.

I have to admit at this stage that I have never actually read the Bible from cover to cover. Yes, I have read extracts, usually when asked to read in church or when trying to make sense of a particular parable. However, I thought it was about time I did read a little of the Apocrypha and see what it was all about.

Firstly, don't be put off by the opening verse of the first book belonging to Tobit, which reads:

The book of the words of Tobit son of Tobiel son of Hananiel son of Aduel son of Gabael son of Raphael son of Raguel of the descendants[a] of Asiel, of the tribe of Naphtali², who in the days of King Shalmaneser[b] of the Assyrians was taken into captivity from Thisbe, which is to the south of Kedesh Naphtali in Upper Galilee, above Asher toward the west, and north of Phogor.

This is certainly not something that you would want to try and articulate in public. But do read on, it's a really interesting story of the time. It tempted me to read further…

More excitement followed with Judith, she turned out to be the 'wonder woman' of Bethulia. Again, her introduction midway through the book left nothing out when it said:

…she was the daughter of Merari son of Ox son of Joseph son of Oziel son of Elkiah son of Ananias son of Gideon son of Raphain son of Ahitub son of Elijah son of Hilkiah son of Eliab son of Nathanael son of Salamiel son of Sarasadai son of Israel.

Another nail-biting tale of the era and not one you would necessarily expect to find in the Bible. Certainly a good read.

The next book belongs to Esther. Now you may have thought that there was a book of Esther in the Old Testament already, and you'd be right. But there the book ends at chapter

10. For some reason, the original Greek version continued with many more books. Why? More research for you! The additional bits fit either before or after sections of the book of Esther as written in the Old Testament. These additions were found in the Greek translations of the original Hebrew.

As you proceed through the Apocrypha, you encounter:

The Wisdom of Solomon
The Book of Sirach
The Book of Baruch
The Letter of Jeremiah
The Prayer of Azariah
The Book of Susanna
The Story of Bel and the Dragon
Maccabees books 1, 2, 3, and 4
Esdras books 1 and 2
The Prayer of Manasseh
Psalm 151

Most include a bevvy of unpronounceable names, lots of history and recognisable connections to what you may have read or heard in the traditional Old Testament books.

No doubt if you entered into the realms of deep ecclesiastical research you would learn of all the answers to the questions the Apocrypha raises. Me, sadly I'm not that committed and just happy to have dipped into it and shared some of my confusion with you.

Enjoy![20]

---

[20] All extracts from the Apocrypha are taken from the 'New Revised Standard Version' of the Bible

Epilogue

How can it be that two books, that I never saw coming, have now landed on the shelves? Looking back, I wonder how this happened and perhaps it just reinforces my belief that "God works in mysterious ways." I had always thought that this expression actually came from the Bible but it seems not to be the case. Looking at its origins, it is more likely to have been a misquote from the hymn, "*God moves in a mysterious way*"[21]. Wherever it came from, He certainly does. When I changed churches some years ago, I was in somewhat of an ecclesiastical wilderness and not quite sure what the future held. Whilst I could not understand what was happening to me at the time, it was obviously meant to be as I was soon welcomed with open arms into another parish, which led my faith to go from strength to strength. Soon after, I was approached to join its lay-led service team and the rest is history. Truly amazing.

I suppose the moral for us all is that whilst at times things may seem dark and foreboding, as they did for me, there will always be a plan for us, which it might take a while to appreciate. Until we see what it is we need faith to see us

---

[21] William Cooper (1731–1800)

through. There will be light at the end of the tunnel even if at times, it just seems to feel like a train coming in the other direction!

Take care, everyone, stay strong, and thank you again for taking the trouble to peruse my musings.

God Bless

Geoff